EXTREME!

Ocean in Motion!

Surfing and the Science of Waves

Paul Mason

Capstone
press

Mankato, Minnesota

Fact Finders is published by Capstone Press,
a Capstone Publishers company.
151 Good Counsel Drive, P.O. Box 669,
Mankato, Minnesota 56002.
www.capstonepress.com

First published 2008

Produced for A & C Black by

Monkey Puzzle Media Ltd
The Rectory, Eyke, Woodbridge
Suffolk IP12 2QW, UK

Library of Congress Cataloging-in-Publication Data

Mason, Paul.
  Ocean in motion! surfing and the science of waves / by
Paul Mason.
    p. cm. -- (Extreme!)
  Includes bibliographical references and index.
  Summary: "Presents the science behind ocean waves and
the sport of surfing"--Provided by publisher.
  ISBN-13: 978-1-4296-3125-9 (hardcover)
  ISBN-10: 1-4296-3125-2 (hardcover)
  ISBN-13: 978-1-4296-3145-7 (pbk.)
  ISBN-10: 1-4296-3145-7 (pbk.)
  1. Ocean waves--Juvenile literature. 2. Ocean currents--
Juvenile literature. 3. Wave-motion, Theory of--Juvenile
literature. I. Title.

GC211.2.M36 2009
551.46'3--dc22

2008025526

Editor: Polly Goodman
Design: Mayer Media Ltd
Picture research: Lynda Lines
Series consultant: Jane Turner

This book is produced using paper that is made from
wood grown in managed, sustainable forests. It is natural,
renewable, and recyclable. The logging and manufacturing
processes conform to the environmental regulations of
the country of origin.

Printed in the United States of America

Picture acknowledgements
Alamy pp. 6 (Jesse Farrar), 23 (Craig Ellenwood); Sylain
Cazenave p. 21; Corbis p. 20 (Clifford White); Getty
Images pp. 22 (Warren Bolster), 24–25 (Sean Davey);
Gary Knights p. 28; Photolibrary.com pp. 8 (Bill Brennan/
Pacific Stock), 9 (Mark Gibson/Index Stock Imagery), 18
(Ron Dahlquist/Pacific Stock), 29 (Carol and Mike
Werner/Phototake Science); Science Photo Library p. 7
(NOAA); Mike Searle pp. 1, 14, 15, 26; Mickey Smith pp.
16, 25 right, 27; Alex Williams pp. 4, 10, 11, 12 both, 13,
17, 19, 24 left; Darrel Wong p. 5.

The front cover shows the Hawaiian surfer Jamie Sterling
at Teahupoo, Tahiti (Alamy/Surfpix).

Every effort has been made to contact copyright holders
of material reproduced in this book. Any omissions will be
rectified in subsequent printings if notice is given to the
publishers.

CONTENTS

Abbreviations km stands for kilometers • **m** stands for meters • **ft** stands for feet •
in stands for inches • **km/h** stands for kilometers per hour • **mph** stands for miles per hour

The biggest ride?

Imagine a wave so big that riding it is like jumping off a house and then having the house chase you down the street! That's just what happened to a lifeguard and surfer called **Darrick Doerner, on January 31, 1988.**

That morning, the waves at Waimea Bay in Hawaii had been just a few feet high. By midafternoon, waves over 23 feet (7 meters) high were rolling into the bay.

The biggest **set** of the day appeared, and Doerner paddled for its biggest wave. His surfboard slid down the huge wall of water, he turned at the bottom, and rode along the wave's **shoulder**. The wave had been over 33 feet (10 meters) tall. It was the biggest wave that anyone had ever paddled their surfboard into.

Some waves are really tall. Others, like the one below, give a long ride.

set group of waves   **shoulder**   part of a wave that has not yet crashed down

4

Surfer Laird Hamilton does a bottom turn on a 30-ft (9-m) wave in Hawaii.

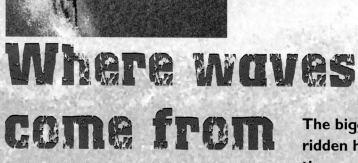

Where waves come from

These gentle waves in Hawaii were made by a storm thousands of miles away.

The biggest wave ever ridden had traveled thousands of miles before it reached Waimea Bay in Hawaii. Surfing waves often travel a long way to get to the beach.

Waves are made by the wind. Strong winds send waves rippling across the surface of the sea, like a bedsheet flicked up so that air goes underneath it.

The stronger the wind, the bigger the waves it produces. The best surfing waves of all are produced by giant storms called **hurricanes**. Serious surfers learn to watch the weather carefully, hoping to see that a storm or hurricane will be sending waves their way!

hurricanes   storms with wind speeds of at least 74 mph (119 km/h)

The biggest wave

In 1933, in the North Pacific, the crew of the *USS Ramapo* spotted the biggest wave ever seen. The wave they saw was a monster 112 feet (34 meters) high—as tall as a seven-story building!

High winds around eye of storm

Wind whips up waves on surface of water.

Waves travel away from storm—and toward surfers!

eye the center of a storm

A satellite photo of Hurricane Dean, taken on August 20, 2007.

Friend and foe

Waves are exciting to ride, but they can also be deadly dangerous. On December 26, 2004, a giant tsunami wave hit the coasts of Southeast Asia. In some places, the tsunami was three times as tall as the biggest wave ever ridden. Nearly a quarter of a million people were killed.

Even waves much smaller than the tsunami cause damage. In fact, waves are constantly wearing away at coastlines. In some countries, people even find their garden and house falling into the sea as a result.

The streets of Phuket, in Thailand, flooded with water from the December 2004 tsunami.

The village that fell into the sea

In 1917, the fishing village of Hallsands, in Devon, United Kingdom, was hit by a terrible storm. The waves swept through the village, wrecking it. Today, most of its buildings still lie under the ocean.

tsunami   a giant wave caused by an earthquake

*Coastal **erosion** at Sandy Bluff, California.*

In the next few months, these houses will fall into the ocean.

CLIFF

CLIFF

CLIFF

WAVES

WAVES

WAVES

Waves eat away at a cliff, causing erosion.

erosion   the wearing away of rock or soil

How waves break

Although waves look like moving water, for most of a wave's life it hardly moves any water at all! How is this possible?

Surfing waves are actually waves of **energy**, traveling away from the storm that caused them. These **pulses** of energy travel across the surface of the ocean. The water moves up and down as the energy passes but is left behind in the same place. Only the energy moves on.

Surfers try to catch waves as they break. This is the moment when the wave's energy is released.

Only when the waves reach the beach do they start to move water forward. As the wave hits shallower water, it slows down. Because the base of the wave is nearer the seabed, it is in shallower water than the top of the wave so it slows down more. The top of the wave spills over, or "breaks."

energy   power, or the ability to do work   **pulses**   beats, or throbs

When waves break

Waves generally break when the water beneath them is 1.3 times their own height. So a 6.5-foot (2-meter) wave breaks in water that is 9 feet (2.7 meters) deep, and so on.

ENERGY

Energy from a distant storm travels across the surface of the ocean.

DEEP WATER

As waves hit shallower water, they start to break. Water tumbles down from the top of the wave to the bottom.

SHALLOW WATER

Catching a wave

Surfers only have a split second to catch a wave as it breaks. Yet just learning to stand up on a surfboard is about as hard as standing on a log in a river, never mind catching a wave at the right time.

1. The surfer paddles hard, trying to get his board moving almost as fast as the wave.

2. As the wave pushes the board to the beach, the surfer pushes down on the deck and whips his feet up.

To make learning easier, beginner surfers look for particular kinds of wave. The best waves for learning break slowly and gently. The **peak** crumbles down the **face** instead of being thrown forward. Because waves like this are less powerful and slower moving, beginners have more time to experiment and learn.

3. He stands up and starts to turn the board along the wave.

Surfer turns this way.

peak the spot where wave first breaks   **face** unbroken front of wave

Turning

Once you've mastered standing up and catching a wave, the next thing you learn is turning. This is like standing on a log in a river ... on one leg!

Snappy turns at the top of the wave always score highly in surfing contests. The judges like to see a bit of spray!

It's impossible to get a good long ride on a wave without doing turns. A typical ride goes like this:

1. Paddle for the wave, which throws you forward.

2. Stand up.

3. Turn at the bottom of the wave and come back up to the top.

4. Turn at the top and get thrown back down.

5. Repeat until blissfully happy.

Which foot forward?

Standing with your left foot forward on the board makes you a "regular foot." Right-foot-forward makes you a "goofy foot."

Surfer Yassine Ramdani makes a right turn on a slow, rolling wave in northern Morocco.

Weight on back foot

Shoulders and arms twist right.

Surfer turns up wave.

Surfer straightens out, with weight off back foot.

This surfer is a regular foot.

Welcome to the Green Room

The "Green Room" is a surfing name for the space inside a tubing wave, like the one on the right. Most surfers never get to enter the Green Room—but that doesn't stop them from trying!

Tubing waves are among the most dangerous ones to ride. They tube because they break on a steep, shallow seabed. The water in front of a wave like the one on the right might only be 3 or 6 feet (1 or 2 meters) deep. If surfers fall, or "wipe out," they can hit the seabed hard.

Oh, man!

Wipeouts on tubing waves can be very painful.

tubing wave   wave that forms a tube of air inside as it breaks   **wipeouts**   falls or crashes

Lip thrown out in front of wave.

Only the tail and **rail** of board bite into wave face.

Shallow water

Surfer makes rapid progress this way!

Teetering on the brink of a painful wipeout, surfer Spencer Hargraves races through the Green Room.

Surfing strummer

Musician Jack Johnson is a talented surfer. He had his front teeth knocked out at the age of 17, while surfing the famous tubing waves at Pipeline, Hawaii.

lip   the breaking tip of a wave   **rail**   edge of surfboard

17

Riding big waves

Big-wave surfers are probably the ones other surfers admire most. It takes a lot of courage to paddle your board into a wave as tall as a house!

*Big-wave surfing in Hawaii. Many big-wave spots are a long way **offshore**.*

One of the problems for big-wave surfers is that the bigger a wave is, the faster it is moving. This is because big waves break in deep water, so they are not slowed down much by a shallow bottom. It is hard to get your board moving fast enough to catch big waves.

Catching big waves is made even harder by what seems like wind. This is caused by air rushing up the wave's face.

offshore   out to sea

gravity force that attracts objects to each other

Tow-in surfing

Tow-in surfing is the most revved-up kind of surfing there is! These surfers use jet skis to give them a high-speed tow into the world's biggest waves.

Until tow-in surfing was invented, the biggest waves went unridden. These giant waves, some over 50 feet (15 meters) tall, break far out at sea. They are traveling so fast that no surfer could paddle his or her board quickly enough to catch them. Then someone realized that a tow from a jet ski would let surfers zoom along at up to 25 miles per hour (40 kilometers per hour)—fast enough to catch much bigger waves.

A jet ski tows the surfer up to speed. The surfer then lets go of the towline and catches the wave.

jet skis   water craft like motorcycles but with a propeller instead of wheels

Surfer Laird Hamilton rides the wave known as "Jaws," in Maui, after a tow from a jet ski. The waves at Maui, in Hawaii, are famous around the world.

Helicopter tow-in

Some surfers have taken tow-in surfing a step further. Amazingly, they have started using helicopters to get a tow into the wave!

"Impact zone," where wave smashes down.

Tow-in surfer's feet are attached to the board with foot straps to help prevent wipeouts.

Tow-in surfboard has heavy, lead center, to stop it from taking off.

Jet skis wait in a safe area, in case the surfer has to be rescued.

21

Wiping out

Wipeout is a surfing word for falling off your surfboard. You might think that falling on to water would not hurt. But it does!

Aieeee!

The science of surfing in (painful) action.

Imagine someone throwing a bucketful of water at your face. It would hurt! Next, imagine how many bucketfuls of water there are in even a little wave. Now maybe you can see why wipeouts can be painful!

Surfing's secret words

Surfers have a name for being swirled round and round by a wave. They call it "the washing machine!"

ARRR! Gravity begins its work, pulling the surfer downward.

Wham! Surfer hits the water and skids along the surface.

Uh-oh! Surfer sucked back up into **curl** of wave. Whole process starts again.

curl the curve of a wave

Water like concrete

Aaaah!

Most people think of water as soft, something you can easily slide into. But if you hit water hard enough, it feels more like concrete.

When you hit the water's surface after a bad wipeout, you're traveling at high speed. The wave throws you forward, toward the beach, and gravity pulls you down. Your body doesn't drop through the surface and under water. Instead it skids along, like a stone skimming along the surface. Only after a few spins in what surfers call the "washing machine" do you sink down and escape the wave's clutches!

Ouch!

"I came up, and something was hitting me in the back of the head. I thought, 'What's that hitting me in the back of the head?' Then I looked round, and it was my foot."
—Hawaiian surfer Titus Kinimaka describes the effects of a **REALLY** bad wipeout.

Brr! Ice-cold surfing

Surfing the far north

Today, there are surfers as far north as Alaska and Scandinavia. Even with the warmest wetsuit, they only manage to stay in the water for half an hour at a time!

Every year, there are more and more surfers in the water. Sometimes, the only way to escape the crowds is to surf in freezing-cold water, where few others dare to go.

Where there ARE big crowds, surfing's rules are very simple:

- The surfer nearest the peak has the right to catch the wave.

- On an unbroken wave, the first person to their feet gets the wave.

- A surfer riding in has to avoid people paddling out.

To avoid crowds like this, some surfers have begun to explore the surf in cold parts of the world such as Alaska, Iceland, and Scandinavia.

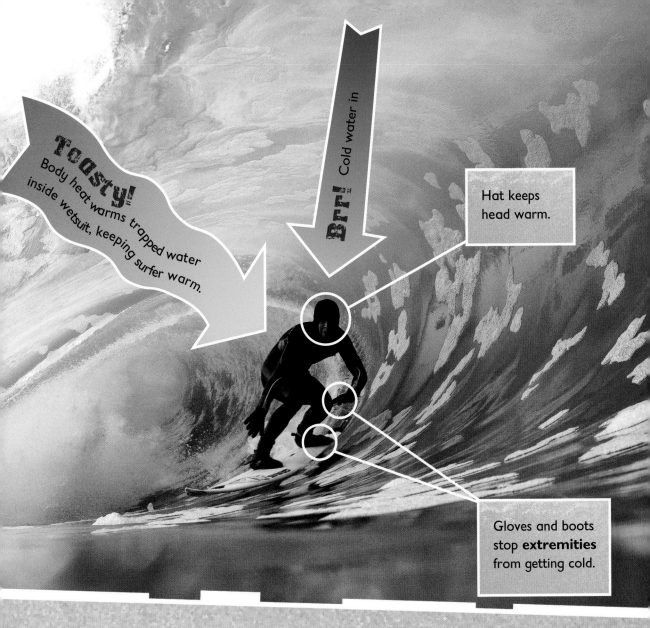

Toasty!
Body heat warms trapped water inside wetsuit, keeping surfer warm.

Brr! Cold water in

Hat keeps head warm.

Gloves and boots stop **extremities** from getting cold.

Today, some surfers choose to avoid the crowds by going to places where the water and air are cold. This means they have to have some special cold-water equipment in their bag!

This surfer, in Ireland, is wearing a full winter surfing kit.

extremities parts of the body that stick out from the torso, especially the hands and the feet

Ripped away

Every year, some surfers are killed in accidents. Understanding the currents caused by waves might stop you from being one of the casualties.

With big surf like this on the beach, there will be lots of water trying to escape back out to sea. This causes strong, dangerous rip currents.

Waves cause movements of water called rip currents (rips), or undertows. These fast-moving flows of water can quickly drag surfers and swimmers out to sea. Rips form in places where the seabed is deeper than the bed on either side of it.

currents flows of water

Fortunately, if you are a confident swimmer it's possible to escape a rip current. Keep calm. Look toward the shore to see if anyone has seen that you need help. If so, wave both arms above your head—the international signal for "HELP!"

Swim ACROSS the current. Most rips are quite narrow, and you should soon escape its clutches. Once you are out of the current, start swimming back to shore. If you find yourself back in the current, swim sideways again.

No waves break where seabed is deeper. Water escapes as a strong rip current.

WATER IN

WATER RUSHES OUT ALONG RIP CURRENT

WATER IN

Swim sideways to escape current.

Glossary

curl the curve of a wave

currents flows of water

energy power, or the ability to do work

erosion the wearing away of rock or soil. Waves erode the coast in some places and then currents carry the worn-away rock or soil along the coast and leave it elsewhere.

extremities parts of the body that stick out from the torso, especially the hands and the feet

eye (of a storm) the center of a storm, where there is no wind and the weather is calm

face the unbroken front of a wave. Surfers aim to ride on the face, as close to the breaking part of the wave as possible.

gravity force that attracts objects to each other

hurricanes storms with wind speeds of at least 74 mph (119 km/h)

jet skis water craft like motorcycles but with a propeller instead of wheels

lip the breaking tip of a wave

offshore out to sea

peak the spot where a wave first breaks. Surfers cluster round the the peak because from there they can get the longest, most exciting rides.

pulses beats, or throbs

rail edge of surfboard

set a group of waves. Surfing myths say that the seventh wave in a set is the best one.

shoulder part of a wave that has not yet crashed down

tsunami a giant wave caused by an earthquake

tubing wave wave that forms a tube of air inside as it breaks

wipeouts falls or crashes

Further information

Books

To The Limit: Surfing by Paul Mason (Raintree-Steck Vaughn, 2001) Great coverage of the basics of surfing, from choosing a board to key techniques.

The Encyclopedia of Surfing by Matt Warshaw (Harcourt, 2003) A book for grown-ups, really, but made up of thousands of fascinating little snippets about every aspect of surfing you can think of.

Magazines

There are loads of good surfing magazines. American magazines include ***Surfing***, ***Surfer***, and ***The Surfers Journal*** (the Journal is expensive, though!). Australian mags include ***ASL*** and ***Tracks***. The best British magazines are ***Carve*** and ***The Surfer's Path***.

Web sites

FactHound offers a safe, fun way to find Internet sites related to this book. All of the sites on FactHound have been researched by our staff.
Visit *www.facthound.com* for age-appropriate sites. You may browse subjects by clicking on letters, or by clicking on pictures and words. **FactHound will fetch the best sites for you!**

Index